D0777137

Patterns of Happiness

KAHLIL
PATTERNS OF HAPPINESS
GIBRAN

Thoughts
on the Joys of Living
Selected
by Ben W. Whitley
Illustrated
by George Kauffman

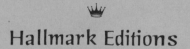

Hallmark Editions

PATTERNS OF HAPPINESS

The earth
is like a beautiful bride
who needs no man-made jewels
to heighten her loveliness
but is content
with the green verdure
of her fields,
and the golden sands
of her seashores,
and the precious stones
on her mountains.

Humanity
is a brilliant river
singing its way
and carrying with it
the mountain's secrets
into the heart of the sea.

We may change
with the seasons,
but the seasons
will not change us.

The just is close
to the people's hearts,
but the merciful
is close to the heart of God.

My thought
is a tender leaf
that sways
in every direction
and finds pleasure
in its swayings.

A tree grown in a cave
does not bear fruit.

Life is an island
in an ocean of loneliness,
an island whose rocks are hopes,
whose trees are dreams,
whose flowers solitude.

The whole earth
is my birthplace
and all humans
are my brothers.

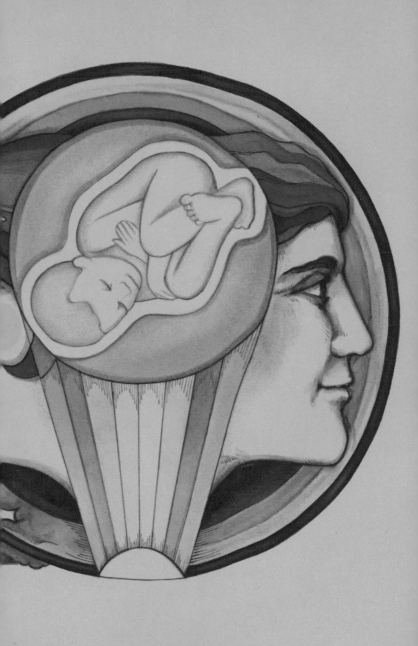

Perplexity
is the beginning
of knowledge.

Does the song
of the sea
end at the shore
or in the hearts
of those who listen to it?

Tomorrow
never leaves a secret
in the book of Eternity.

Now I realize
that the trees blossom
in Spring
and bear fruit
in Summer
without seeking praise,
and they
drop their leaves
in Autumn
and become naked
in Winter
without fearing blame.

Beauty is
that which attracts
the soul,
and that which
loves to give
and not to receive.

In one drop of water
are found the secrets
of all the endless oceans.

He who has not looked
on Sorrow will never see Joy.

In the depth of my soul,
there is a wordless song.

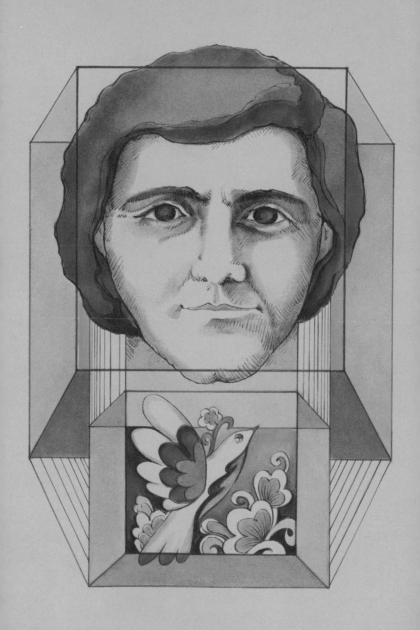

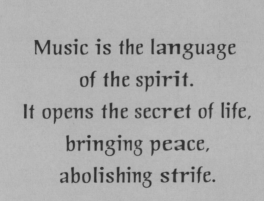

Music is the language
of the spirit.
It opens the secret of life,
bringing peace,
abolishing strife.

Our appearance,
our words,
our actions
are never greater
than ourselves.
For the soul
is our house;
our eyes its windows;
and our words
its messengers.

Which one of us
listens to the hymn
of the brook
when the tempest speaks?

Glorious intoxication
of the soul is the reward
of all who seek it
in the bosom of Nature.

God has given
to each of us
a spirit with wings,
wings on which to soar
into the spacious firmament
of Love and Freedom.

Set in York, a calligraphic roman face
designed for the Visual Graphics Corporation.
Typography by Hallmark Photo Composition.
Printed in specially selected match colors
on Gold Sonata Vellum by Hopper.
Designed by Jay D. Johnson.